★ ★ ★ ★ ★ ★ ★ ★ ★ ★ ★ ★ ★ ★

NITRO CIRCUS

D0913251

BEST OF

FMX

RIPLEY

PUBLISHING

a Jim Pattison Company

THE BIRTH OF FREESTYLE MOTOCROSS

TRICKS & FLIPS ON A MOTOCROSS BIKE

FMX stands for freestyle motocross. It's an action sport that's a blend of BMX freestyle and motocross. Motocross is motorcycle racing on off-road, usually dirt, courses. BMX freestyle is a sport of tricks, whips, and flips on dirt bicycles. Do those same tricks on a motorcycle and you have FMX!

FMX riders perform freestyle tricks, jumps, and other stunts on specially modified motocross bikes. FMX was born in the 1990s, based on the wicked foundation of motocross racing and its dedicated athletes.

When motocross athletes saw what was happening in the BMX action sports world, it was just a matter of time until they got their own piece of the action! Their stunts are judged based on difficulty level, precision, height, and variation of tricks.

Travis Pastrana is not only the father of Nitro Circus but also one of the most decorated FMX athletes in the history of the sport.

FMX has been part of the X Games since 1999. This first FMX event was won by Travis Pastrana.

Freestyle motocross originally began in the hills of Southern California, with riders using the natural terrain to execute tricks.

A constant progression of bike modifications, ramps, landers, and tricks makes FMX one of the most innovative and dynamic disciplines in action sports.

In 2002, Caleb Wyatt became the first motocross rider to land a backflip. This feat changed the course of FMX forever.

GET IN ON THE FMX ACTION!

HORSEPOWERED JUMPS AND TRICKS TO BLOW YOUR MIND

Whether it's the double frontflip, landed for the first time in competition by Gregg Duffy in 2016 at the Nitro World Games, or the cliffhanger backflip, or even the double backflip Superman, there's no doubt that FMX is an action sport to rival the best! It's broken into two main categories—big air and freestyle motocross.

DID YOU KNOW?

First held in 2016 and created by Nitro Circus, the Nitro World Games is an international action sport competition. Athletes in BMX, FMX, scooter, rallycross, inline skating, and skateboarding compete for trophies. In just a few years, these games have seen many broken records and world's firsts!

ENNETT'S WAR
In Theatres August 30

DJI

BELL

NITRO WORLD GAMES

BIG AIR FMX

Riders jump from dirt and metal ramps that are often longer than 75 feet! Their jumps are judged on style, difficulty, and originality. Best-known tricks include the Superman, the body varial, the Hart attack, the cliffhanger, and the backflip.

CLIFFHANGER BACK FLIP

FREESTYLE MOTOCROSS

Riders perform routines while riding along a course, which lasts from 60 to 90 seconds, doing multiple jumps of varying lengths and angles. They are judged on difficulty, originality, and style.

SUPERMAN DOUBLE SEAT GRAB

ANATOMY OF AN FMX BIKE

The FMX bike is a souped-up (or slimmed-down) version of a typical motocross bike. The point is to make the bike as light and as responsive as possible, with the goal of improving performance while tricking out.

HANDLEBARS

FMX riders use oversized handlebars so there's more room for over-the-bar tricks, such as the barhop or dead-body tricks.

STEERING STABILIZER

This stabilizer keeps the handlebars straight even when the rider lets go during a no-handed trick. It's mounted below the middle of the handlebar.

REAR SHOCK

Suspension is modified and made stiffer for smoother landings.

FLIP LEVERS

This metal bar wrapped with foam comes off the handlebars and goes in front of the rider's forearm. It stops riders from rotating during flips but lets the bike continue to move. Levers are folded down when not in use so they're out of the way during bar tricks.

GRAB HOLES

These wide holes are cut into the side panels to create an excellent grip point for seat-grab tricks.

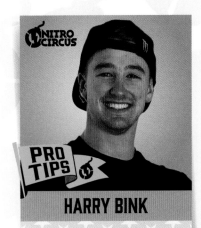

PRO TIPS

HARRY BINK

A lighter bike means less work for the rider, a critical factor in a sport where athletes soar more than 30 feet above the ground and launch distances of 75 feet to execute awe-inspiring tricks.

EXHAUST SYSTEM

Most riders upgrade the standard exhaust system for more power.

FOOT PEGS

Wide foot pegs give riders more stability and help absorb the impact of landing.

FMX BIKE MODS FOR THE REST OF US

TRANSFORM YOUR MOTOCROSS BIKE FOR PERFORMING TRICKS

It's not too difficult to make mods to your stock motocross bike to equip it for amazing tricks! FMX riders make these changes to start with:

Shorten the width of the handlebars to make it easier to put your legs around or over the bars for such tricks as the heel-clicker and barhop.

Add a steering stabilizer to help keep the front tire straight when performing no-handed tricks.

NITRO CIRCUS
PRO TIPS
JOSH SHEEHAN

What's the difference between a 2-stroke and a 4-stroke engine? A 2-stroke engine makes for a lighter, less expensive, and faster bike than a 4-stroke. They are also harder to control and require more maintenance than 4-strokes. Also, a 2-stroke 125 cc engine is the same as a 4-stroke 250 cc. Most newbies begin with 2-stroke bikes, and many pro riders stay with a 2-stroke their entire careers.

Ensure the bike has stiff suspension and good quality tires.

Trim the front number plate and apply grip tape to the front forks for cliffhanger and Lazy Boy tricks.

Shave down the seat foam for wider range of motion and a more secure grip.

Move brakes and clutch cables away from the bars to avoid getting your feet caught on the bike.

Add wider foot pegs for maximum control when jumping and landing.

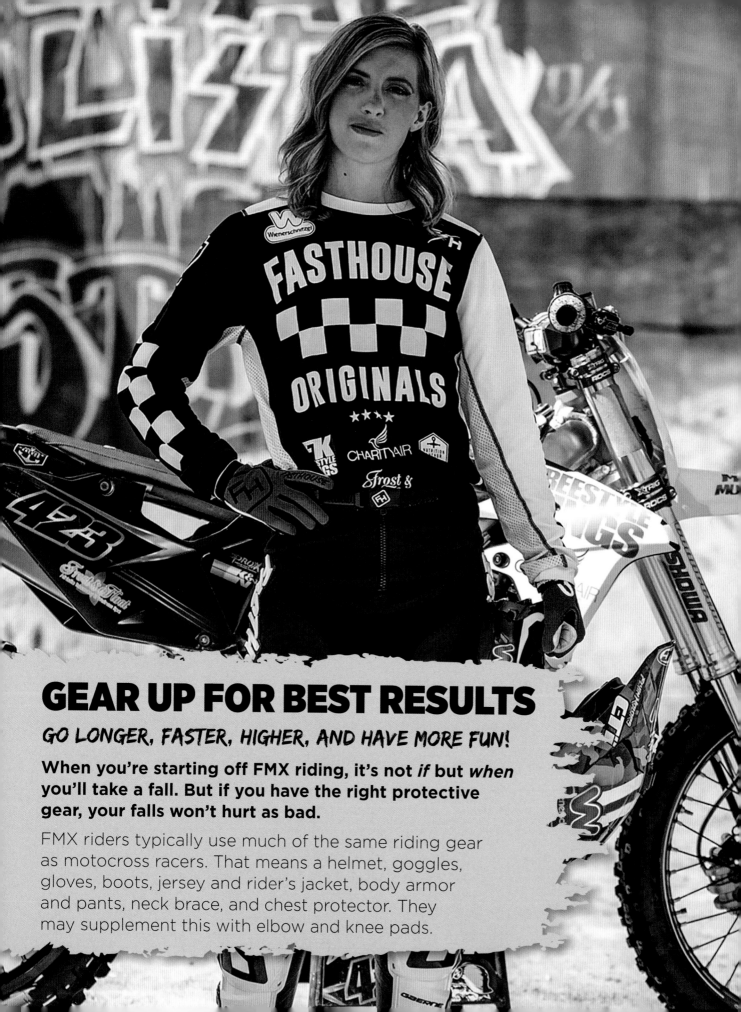

GEAR UP FOR BEST RESULTS

GO LONGER, FASTER, HIGHER, AND HAVE MORE FUN!

When you're starting off FMX riding, it's not *if* but *when* you'll take a fall. But if you have the right protective gear, your falls won't hurt as bad.

FMX riders typically use much of the same riding gear as motocross racers. That means a helmet, goggles, gloves, boots, jersey and rider's jacket, body armor and pants, neck brace, and chest protector. They may supplement this with elbow and knee pads.

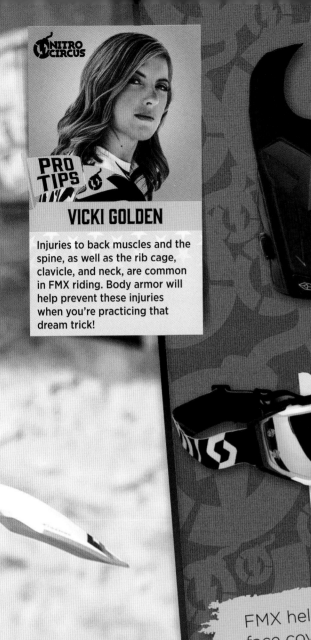

PRO TIPS

VICKI GOLDEN

Injuries to back muscles and the spine, as well as the rib cage, clavicle, and neck, are common in FMX riding. Body armor will help prevent these injuries when you're practicing that dream trick!

Want to look like a futuristic superhero and protect your back and ribs at the same time? Hello, body armor.

Goggles protect your eyes from dirt and provide UV protection from the sun. The better you can see, the better your trick will be!

FMX helmets have full-face coverage and are the same as motocross helmets. They are designed for hard impacts.

Gloves prevent callouses from the bike grips and protect your hands when you fall. These should be snug on your hands.

BREAK RECORDS, NOT BONES

A SAFE RAMP MAKES THE BEST PLAYGROUND

As the pros know, safety isn't just about the gear you wear. Be sure that the landing lengths for your ramps are long enough and you have padding installed on-site. Also, ensure that the landing height, length, and angle for your ramps are correct.

Are the run-in and run-out lengths long enough to accommodate you? No rider wants to land his or her first backflip to then run out straight into a wall.

RAMPS

It's much better to buy the ramp you need rather than trying to build your own. Personally built ramps and makeshift landing areas can cause serious injuries—they aren't long or strong enough to handle the rider or the tricks. Save your money and invest in a proper ramp that meets FMX standards and safety guidelines.

DID YOU KNOW?

If you do plan on building your own ramps, be sure you are using a certified ramp plan (such as the **Rev 1 Ramp Plan**), with industry-agreed-upon specs. Beware, though, it won't be much more expensive to buy one if you make it properly!

EQUIPMENT SAFETY 101

FMX BIKE SAFETY TIPS

Your bike takes a beating when you're mastering tricks. Make sure every part of your bike is tight before you ride! Be sure to give your bike a once-over and check these parts:

BRAKES
Make sure your brakes are working. Check both front and rear for a firm action.

STEERING STABILIZER
Check your steering stabilizer to make sure it hasn't been bent or cracked.

CABLES
Make sure the brake and clutch cables are out of the way to avoid getting your feet caught on the bike.

TIRES
Do your tires need air? FMX tires should be adjusted to the manufacturers' specifications.

HARDWARE
Make sure all the bolts and screws are tight. The jarring jumps and flips can loosen connections over time.

SEAT
Make sure the seat is tightly fastened, free of damage, and positioned correctly.

NITRO CIRCUS

PRO TIPS

HARRY BINK

Be sure to check the course and ramps for any hazards before you begin, especially when it's a homemade ramp or course that isn't sanctioned or maintained by some governing body. Taking a few minutes to check for holes, divots, sharp edges, gaps, and so on will save you lots of pain and potential injury later on.

PROGRESSION THE SMART WAY

FMX SAFETY TIPS

Being safe means more time on the bike and less time on the ground. To start, don't ride above your ability—especially when you're learning new techniques. Before you even try any tricks, make sure you can take off and do a controlled landing on the same spot every time. Ramps are different from dirt; you have to build up to them.

Always start with and master easier tricks before you move on to the advanced ones! A good order of progression is one-footers, no-footers, then one-handers. The most important and most critical first step is to master the basic ramp jump. The pros make it look easy, but it takes practice to know the exact speed, motion, body placement, and momentum you need to successfully jump the ramp time and again.

TRAVIS PASTRANA

Motocross bikes weigh approximately 250 pounds. That's a lot of bike landing on top of you in an epic fail!

Never ride without protecting your head and neck. Concussions are more common in young people than in adults, and despite how common they are, they are still a traumatic brain injury. Don't take any chances: ride smart and wear a helmet that's made for FMX/BMX riding.

START WITH THE BASICS

FMX SKILLS: BUILD A FOUNDATION

In FMX there are basic riding skills that are fundamental to learning everything else, no matter how far you want to take the sport. You have to start by mastering these building blocks in order to be safe and conquer the ramp.

If you want to pull off the seemingly impossible,

you have to start by mastering the fundamentals!

The one-footer is when you remove one leg while in midair during a jump. Before you move your leg, your bike should be level and your weight should be centered. Start by removing your preferred leg off the foot peg 3-4 inches. With practice, you'll be able to make this movement bigger and hold it longer.

ONE-FOOTER

The one-hander requires you to give up a little control over the bike, which can feel strange at first. Start by simply opening your hand off the grip when you're in the air. Then move your hand a little bit farther from the handlebars each time.

ONE-HANDER

DID YOU KNOW?

Practice makes perfect! Being able to remove your hands and feet off the bike confidently is the basis for all the big moves that you see the pros do. How can you do a Superman without knowing how to remove your foot safely from the peg? You need to be able to do these basic tricks flawlessly, consistently, and without fear before you move on to harder things.

CONQUERING THE COMBOS

BUILDING YOUR FMX SKILLS

Once you have the fundamental techniques firmly in hand, you can start building on them, creating your own style, and displaying amazing combos. Master the fundamentals and you'll have a toolbox of tricks to start building with!

By stringing several fundamental tricks together, you can pull off stunning combos!

Here Cam Sinclair sends a backflip no-hander, a more technical version of the backflip and no-hander.

Once you've mastered the one-footer, it's time to learn the no-footer, where you remove both legs off the bike at the same time. Keeping your arms straight and firm, lift both feet off the pedals slightly. Practice until you can start extending your legs out and up farther and farther.

The no-hander is the next step after you can confidently and consistently take one hand off the bike during a jump. The key is to keep the bike level and lean forward over the bars a little as you release your hands. Start with a one-hander and lift the other hand only a few inches from the grip, then build from there.

NO-HANDER

DID YOU KNOW?

Let's talk natural progression. After you've mastered the no-footer and no-hander, you can move on to the can-can or even the nothing (no hands and no feet). How you progress is up to you and what feels comfortable. Remember to always wear safety gear and to progress in small, natural steps. Don't try a new trick until you've mastered the one before it.

COOL AIR TRICKS TO START

FROM THE NAC NAC TO THE DOUBLE NAC

Once you master the one-footer, you can start working on these two tricks: the nac nac and the double nac.

MELLOW

NITRO
METER

TRICK #01

NAC NAC

The nac nac is where you bring one leg and your torso completely off the bike to the opposite side and turn toward the backside of your bike in a twisting motion.

To master this trick, it's best to take your dominant foot off the pedal. (Left-foot-forward riders are usually left-handed, and their dominant side is their left.)

DOUBLE NAC

Here Michael "Chucky" Norris displays the double nac, where both feet are off and pointing perpendicular to the bike on one side.

RADICAL

NITRO METER

THE NAC NAC GROWS UP
BUILDING ON BASIC SKILLS TO PRODUCE POWERFUL TRICKS

Riders use more basic skills like the nac nac as building blocks to show off more impressive tricks.

MELLOW

NITRO
METER

TRICK #03

TOPSIDE NAC

Beau Bamburg performs the topside nac, where the entire bike is sideways, parallel to the ground.

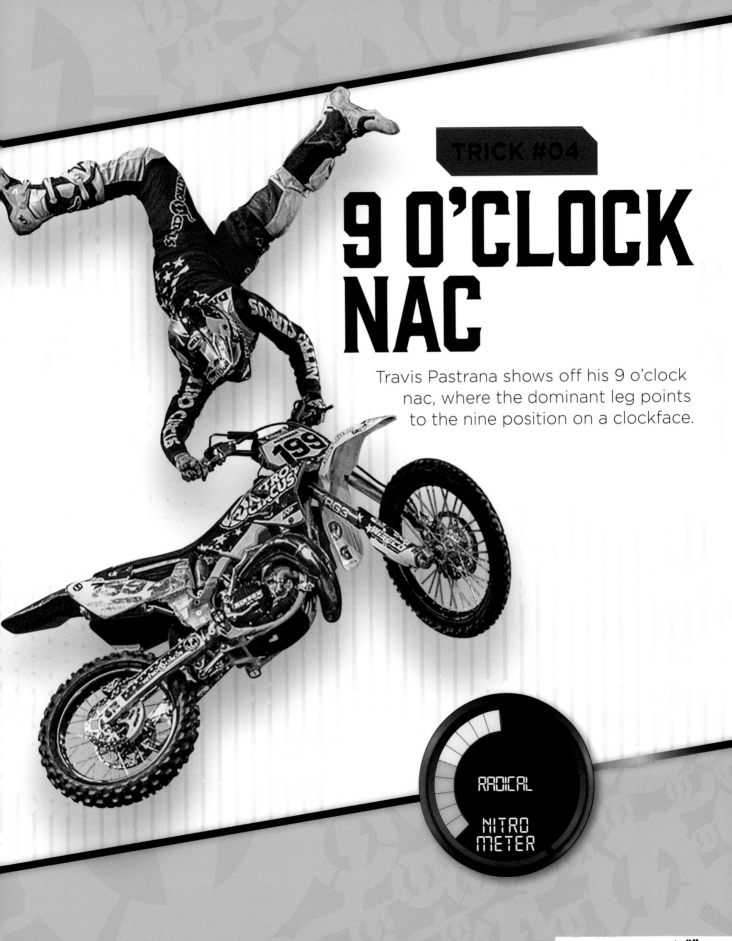

9 O'CLOCK NAC

Travis Pastrana shows off his 9 o'clock nac, where the dominant leg points to the nine position on a clockface.

RADICAL

NITRO METER

SEAT GRABS AND DOUBLE GRABS

SEAT GRABBING AT A NEW LEVEL

In a basic seat grab, the rider takes one hand off the handlebars and grabs the seat, while moving his or her entire body backward behind the bike, in a full extension.

MELLOW

NITRO METER

SEAT GRAB INDY

During a seat grab Indy, Vicki Golden executes a seat grab while kicking her legs in a scissorlike motion, side to side.

DID YOU KNOW?

Adding an "Indy" (from Indian air) to any trick requires the riders to extend their legs and cross them in a scissorlike motion. The bigger the leg extension, the more points awarded.

DOUBLE GRAB

In the double grab, Scott "Topp Dog" Fitzgerald uses both hands and grabs either side (using the grab holes).

RADICAL

NITRO METER

HOLD ON TO YOUR SEAT

GRAB-AND-GO FLIPS AND COMBO TRICKS

With these seat grabs, the rider places both hands on the seat, extends his or her entire body away from the bike, and integrates multiple tricks into a cohesive combination.

TRICK #07

DOUBLE GRAB INDY

Gregg Duffy performs the double grab Indy, where the legs cross while performing the double grab.

RADICAL

NITRO METER

DOUBLE GRAB BACKFLIP

Josh Sheehan shows off his double grab backflip, a perfect example of adding one trick to another for an even more impressive display.

NEXT LEVEL!

NITRO METER

FLIPPING WITH FLAIR

FLIPPING FRENZY

Flips, which are an advanced skill, are when the rider and the bike turn head over heels while airborne. There are many ways that riders add to the basic flip. When you're learning these jaw-dropping moves, it's best to start with a foam pit.

NEXT LEVEL!

NITRO METER

TRICK #09

CORDOVA FLIP

During the flip, riders bring their feet up underneath the bars, press their knees to their chest, and then look upside down out over the back fender. Adam Jones was the first rider to land this trick in competition.

RULER FLIP

Hold your body straight like a ruler, then pull off a flip. That's the ruler flip! Add a scissor twist with your legs and you get the ruler Indy flip.

NEXT LEVEL!

NITRO METER

HEAD OVER HEELS FOR FLIPPING

GET OUT THERE AND FLIP OUT

Flips can be customized by the rider and are often dependent on the ramp size. Flips are the mainstay of FMX ramp displays, and riders enjoy showing off their personalities and their skills by mixing it up.

TRICK #11

HEEL-CLICKER FLIP

Jarryd McNeil performs a heel-clicker flip by taking his feet off the foot pegs and bringing them around the handlebars in front of him, touching his heels together.

NEXT LEVEL!

NITRO METER

NO-HANDS FLIP

Adam Jones's no-hands flip shows off how much arm extension he can get during the middle of the flip.

NEXT
LEVEL!

NITRO
METER

MOVING AROUND ON THE BIKE

INTERMEDIATE TRICKS!

The pros consider these high-flying feats intermediate tricks, and they often increase the difficulty and point values by combining them with other techniques.

TRICK #13

LAZY BOY

The classic Lazy Boy is where the rider lies flat on his or her back along the bike—feet toward the handlebars and head along the back of the bike.

TRICK #14

LAZY BOY BACKFLIP

With a Lazy Boy backflip, during the backflip, the rider lies prone, back flat against the bike, then returns to position before the landing.

HART ATTACK

Gregg Duffy shows off the Hart attack, named after Carey Hart who invented the trick, where the rider points both legs straight up in the air. One hand grabs the seat, while the other holds onto the handlebars.

RADICAL
NITRO METER

ONE-HANDED HART ATTACK

With the one-handed Hart attack, only one hand is holding the seat; the other is pointed upward along the legs. Michael "Chucky" Norris makes it look easy.

EXTREME
NITRO METER

PRO TRICKS

CONTORTIONS IN ALL DIRECTIONS

Some tricks are so "tricky" that even by themselves they take an enormous amount of skill, practice, and courage to master. These are a few of the revered pro, advanced tricks.

TRICK #17

SHAOLIN

The Shaolin, showcased here by Clinton Moore, requires riders to do a barhop by jumping over the handlebars and then spread their legs apart in a V while in front of the bike.

RADICAL

NITRO METER

SHAOLIN BACKFLIP

The Shaolin backflip requires riders to pull off a Shaolin move during the course of the backflip. How do they know which way is up?

NEXT LEVEL!
NITRO METER

WHIPS AND BODY VARIALS
TWISTING AND TURNING IN AIR

Turning and twisting horizontally, with the bike or without it, requires courage and skill. You have to have enough confidence to make it all the way around. Pros do it with style.

WHIP

A whip is when the rider whips the bike sideways so that it swings out at least 90 degrees from the rider's body. This is Vicki Golden doing a whip turndown.

RADICAL

NITRO METER

TRICK #20

VAULT

Body varials like this vault have the riders coming off the bike into a twist, turning a full 360 degrees back into position while the bike itself does not twist or turn.

NEXT LEVEL! NITRO METER

UP, UP, AND AWAY!

SOAR LIKE SUPERMAN

The Superman is one of the most recognized air tricks in action sports. In midair, the rider lifts both feet off the pedals and pushes them back behind him or her, parallel to the ground, resembling Superman flying. Some say it dates back to 1987, but others say it has been around informally as long as athletes have been jumping ramps. The pros often add other tricks while performing the Superman in order to maximize their scores—not to mention the wow factor. Here are just a few variations.

TRICK #21

NO-HAND SUPERMAN

Some riders, like Josh Sheehan here, can even let go of the bike completely for a few seconds, and this is called the no-hand Superman.

RADICAL

NITRO METER

TRICK #22

RULER

As Vicki Golden demonstrates, a ruler is basically a handstand over your handlebars while trying to keep your body as straight as possible.

EXTREME

NITRO METER

KISS OF DEATH

Can you do a backflip? Can you do the kiss of death? Imagine doing both at the same time, and then adding a second backflip! The kiss of death double backflip is a trick that you have to see to believe. Only the pros can pull this off. Josh Sheehan's perfect rendition earned him 2nd place in FMX Best Trick at the 2018 Nitro World Games.

NEXT LEVEL! NITRO METER

The kiss of death (KOD) is when the rider basically does a handstand on the bike, putting his or her head toward the front fender, as if to kiss it, while being upside down. Josh Sheehan is one of the only athletes who performs this trick, or any double-backflip combos, on a regular basis.

Kevlar.

NITRO WORLD GAMES

THE CLIFFHANGER

HANGING ON BY A TOE

While in the air, the rider stands straight up on the bike and catches the underside of his or her handlebars with their feet. The more the arms and body extend upward, the better the trick. That's the cliffhanger.

CLIFFHANGER

Riders catch the bike with the inside of their feet, gripping around the top of the front fork to give maximum control. That way, they can add on flips, twists, and grabs to this already impressive display.

EXTREME

NITRO METER

CLIFFHANGER BACKFLIP

Talk about progression. The cliffhanger backflip requires the rider to take two tough tricks and pull them off together in one smooth move. Adam Jones makes it look easy.

NEXT LEVEL!

NITRO METER

Travis Pastrana was born in Annapolis, Maryland, and at four years old was already riding a one-speed motorcycle. Despite excelling in mountain biking and his studies (graduating from high school three years early), he knew motorsports were his calling from early on—winning five Loretta Lynn National Amateur crowns beginning in 1992, plus a handful of Canadian titles for good measure. In 1998, the then 14-year-old captured the world freestyle championship. But he was just getting started.

"I won the first pro race I ever entered (125 cc) and also won a gold medal in freestyle at X Games, even though I was the youngest person there," Pastrana recalls. Travis continued to display his versatility into the early 2000s, racking up numerous supercross and motocross podiums, as well as a Motocross of Nations Championship title. In 2001, Travis was awarded Motocross Rider of the Year at the ESPN Action Sports & Music Awards.

He has since accumulated 17 X Games medals, including 11 gold medals, plus five golds from the Gravity Games, and more wins at other events, including Dew Tour and Red Bull XFighters.

SPOTLIGHT ON
TRAVIS PASTRANA

BORN: 10-8-83 **HOME:** Annapolis, MD ⊙ @travispastrana

WORLD'S FIRST

At the 2006 X Games, Travis redefined what was possible in FMX with his groundbreaking double backflip on a motorbike. ESPN highlighted the historic world's first in a 2014 twentieth anniversary X Games celebration, and the city of Los Angeles named it one of the greatest moments in STAPLES Center history (alongside L.A. Lakers and Kings championships, and sold-out concerts by U2, Garth Brooks, and more). As the ringleader of Nitro Circus, Travis is committed to the progression of action sports as a whole.

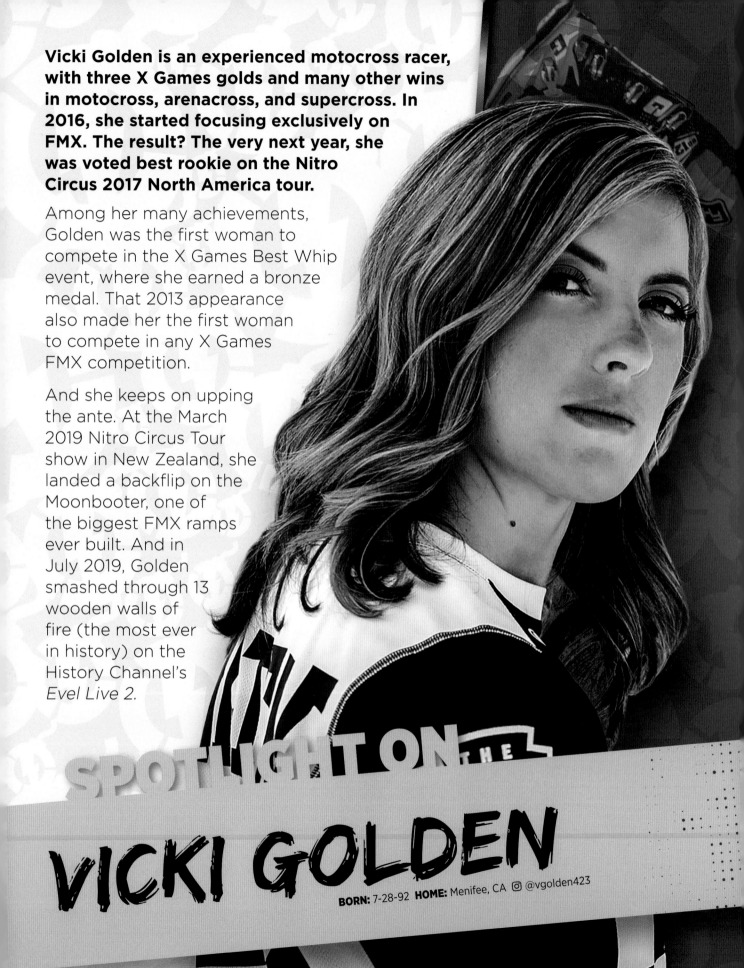

Vicki Golden is an experienced motocross racer, with three X Games golds and many other wins in motocross, arenacross, and supercross. In 2016, she started focusing exclusively on FMX. The result? The very next year, she was voted best rookie on the Nitro Circus 2017 North America tour.

Among her many achievements, Golden was the first woman to compete in the X Games Best Whip event, where she earned a bronze medal. That 2013 appearance also made her the first woman to compete in any X Games FMX competition.

And she keeps on upping the ante. At the March 2019 Nitro Circus Tour show in New Zealand, she landed a backflip on the Moonbooter, one of the biggest FMX ramps ever built. And in July 2019, Golden smashed through 13 wooden walls of fire (the most ever in history) on the History Channel's *Evel Live 2.*

SPOTLIGHT ON THE

VICKI GOLDEN

BORN: 7-28-92 **HOME:** Menifee, CA ⓘ @vgolden423

Golden nearly lost her right foot due to a freestyle accident at a January 2018 show. She was off the bike for nearly a year and endured seven surgeries, only to come back and land a backflip off the massive Moonbooter ramp!

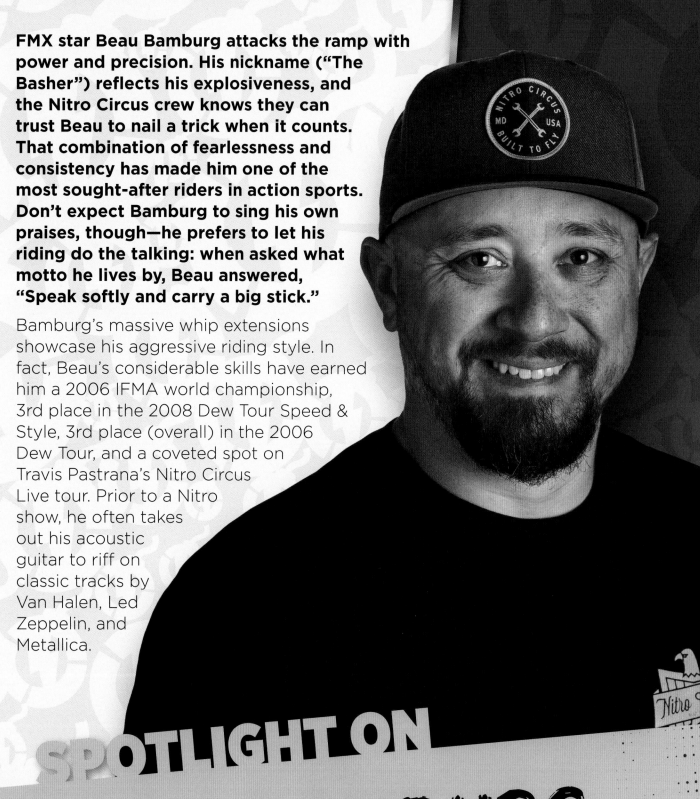

FMX star Beau Bamburg attacks the ramp with power and precision. His nickname ("The Basher") reflects his explosiveness, and the Nitro Circus crew knows they can trust Beau to nail a trick when it counts. That combination of fearlessness and consistency has made him one of the most sought-after riders in action sports. Don't expect Bamburg to sing his own praises, though—he prefers to let his riding do the talking: when asked what motto he lives by, Beau answered, "Speak softly and carry a big stick."

Bamburg's massive whip extensions showcase his aggressive riding style. In fact, Beau's considerable skills have earned him a 2006 IFMA world championship, 3rd place in the 2008 Dew Tour Speed & Style, 3rd place (overall) in the 2006 Dew Tour, and a coveted spot on Travis Pastrana's Nitro Circus Live tour. Prior to a Nitro show, he often takes out his acoustic guitar to riff on classic tracks by Van Halen, Led Zeppelin, and Metallica.

SPOTLIGHT ON

BEAU BAMBURG

BORN: 3-7-78 **HOME:** Gresham, OR @beaubam612

Creator of the Instagram sensation #WhipItWednesday, Beau can throw a whip longer than almost anyone else in FMX, throwing his bike out to one side while flying through the air and holding the trick until the last possible second.

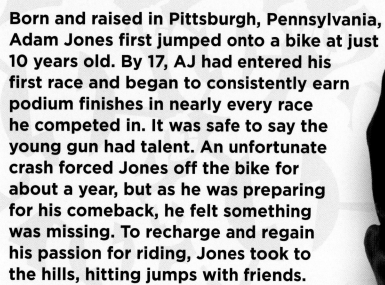

Born and raised in Pittsburgh, Pennsylvania, Adam Jones first jumped onto a bike at just 10 years old. By 17, AJ had entered his first race and began to consistently earn podium finishes in nearly every race he competed in. It was safe to say the young gun had talent. An unfortunate crash forced Jones off the bike for about a year, but as he was preparing for his comeback, he felt something was missing. To recharge and regain his passion for riding, Jones took to the hills, hitting jumps with friends.

The experiment worked, and before long Adam devoted himself to FMX full-time. By 2007, he had won his first X Games gold medal. Jones has since taken home five more X Games medals (four silver and one bronze). Jones has moved FMX forward with a series of unbelievable world's firsts. Besides innovating and inventing new tricks, Jones is also known for his technical precision, throwing considerable extension into his tricks. With such a tremendous resumé, Adam Jones is undoubtedly one of the most exciting FMX athletes on the planet.

SPOTLIGHT ON

ADAM JONES

BORN: 7-23-84 **HOME:** Pittsburgh, PA ⊙ @adamjones760

6 ✖ GAMES MEDALS | 1 🌐 NITRO WORLD GAMES TROPHY

AJ has been credited for inventing many tricks, including the Cordova flip, Shaolin backflip, and the dead-body flip.

As a kid, Gregg Duffy wanted nothing more than to race professional motocross. Growing up in the same area of Maryland as Travis Pastrana, Gregg naturally looked up to Travis and wanted to follow in his footsteps by racing amateur motocross and eventually professional motocross.

Gregg started riding dirt bikes at eight years old and went on to race at many amateur nationals. Chasing success in professional motocross can be an expensive and difficult task. At 26 years old, Gregg decided to shift focus to a newfound passion: freestyle motocross.

SPOTLIGHT ON

GREGG DUFFY

BORN: 4-27-89 **HOME:** Bowie, MD 🄾 @motoduff

WORLD'S FIRST

In early 2016, Gregg was fully invested in FMX, working to perfect his skills and attempting to land the world's first FMX double frontflip. The last athlete to try this trick, Nitro's own Bruce Cook, wound up paralyzed from the waist down from a horrific crash during his attempt. Gregg spent countless hours learning how to best execute this monumental trick, and in July 2016, he unveiled it to the world at the inaugural Nitro World Games. With thousands watching in the stands and millions tuned-in from home, Gregg landed the world's first double frontflip on a motorcycle.

Fan-favorite Blake "Bilko" Williams was born and raised in Baxter, Australia, just outside of Melbourne. A true innovator, Bilko was the first international rider to win an X Games Freestyle gold in 2009 and has several world's first credits to his name. Like many FMX riders, Bilko started out his riding career racing motocross and BMX. In 2003, Bilko turned pro in racing and also performed in his first FMX show. Just one year later, Bilko embarked on his professional FMX career.

With six X Games medals that range from Best Trick in 2006 to Speed & Style in 2015, Bilko has quite the resumé. He took the gold at the Dew Tour in 2008 and just one year later in 2009 was crowned the Transworld FMX Rider of the Year. While practice, competitiveness, and fitness are essential for the success of any FMX rider, the ability to travel the world with his friends is something that Bilko enjoys the most.

SPOTLIGHT ON
BLAKE WILLIAMS

BORN: 4-4-85 **HOME:** Baxter, AU 📷 @bilkofmx

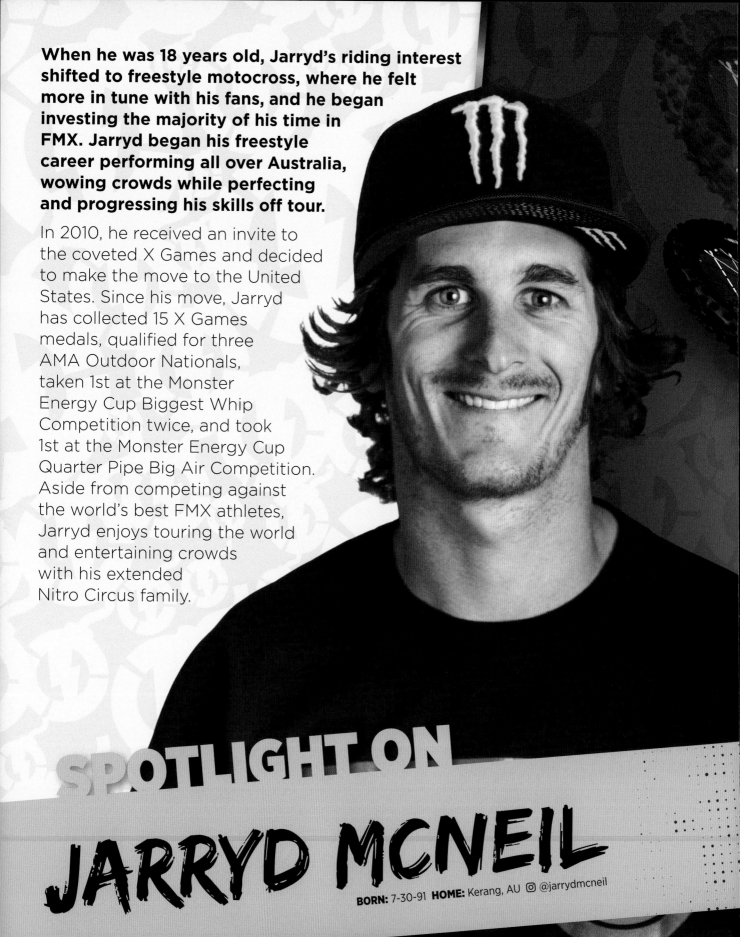

When he was 18 years old, Jarryd's riding interest shifted to freestyle motocross, where he felt more in tune with his fans, and he began investing the majority of his time in FMX. Jarryd began his freestyle career performing all over Australia, wowing crowds while perfecting and progressing his skills off tour.

In 2010, he received an invite to the coveted X Games and decided to make the move to the United States. Since his move, Jarryd has collected 15 X Games medals, qualified for three AMA Outdoor Nationals, taken 1st at the Monster Energy Cup Biggest Whip Competition twice, and took 1st at the Monster Energy Cup Quarter Pipe Big Air Competition. Aside from competing against the world's best FMX athletes, Jarryd enjoys touring the world and entertaining crowds with his extended Nitro Circus family.

SPOTLIGHT ON

JARRYD MCNEIL

BORN: 7-30-91 **HOME:** Kerang, AU 🄾 @jarrydmcneil

At the 2019 X Games in Minneapolis, McNeil set a record by winning his fourth X Games gold in a row in the Moto X Step-Up competition. He cleared the 40-foot bar to take home the gold.

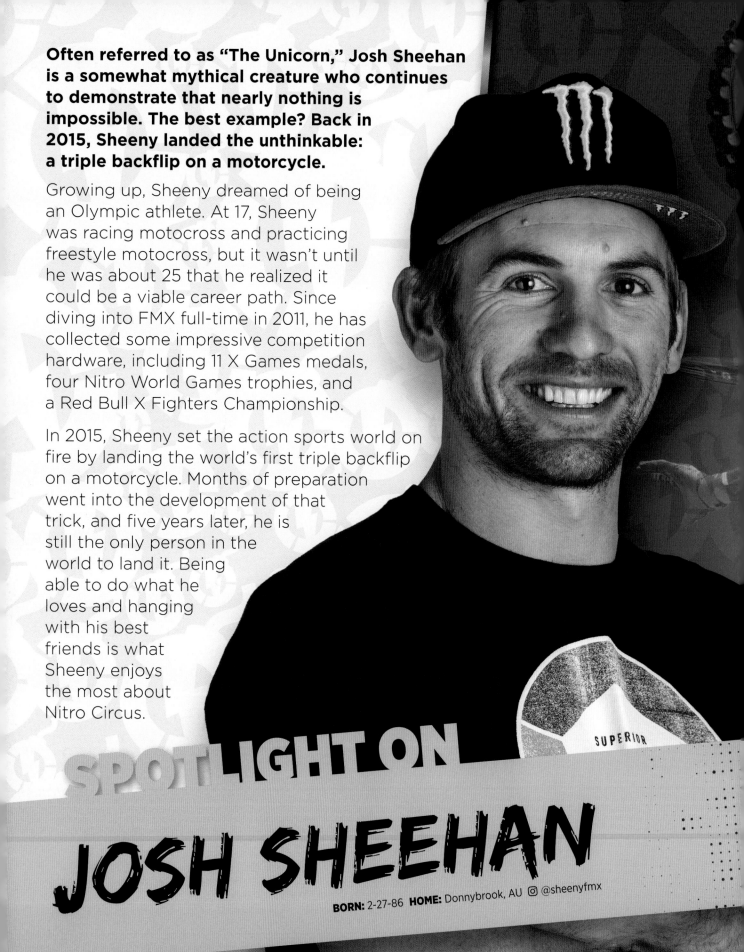

Often referred to as "The Unicorn," Josh Sheehan is a somewhat mythical creature who continues to demonstrate that nearly nothing is impossible. The best example? Back in 2015, Sheeny landed the unthinkable: a triple backflip on a motorcycle.

Growing up, Sheeny dreamed of being an Olympic athlete. At 17, Sheeny was racing motocross and practicing freestyle motocross, but it wasn't until he was about 25 that he realized it could be a viable career path. Since diving into FMX full-time in 2011, he has collected some impressive competition hardware, including 11 X Games medals, four Nitro World Games trophies, and a Red Bull X Fighters Championship.

In 2015, Sheeny set the action sports world on fire by landing the world's first triple backflip on a motorcycle. Months of preparation went into the development of that trick, and five years later, he is still the only person in the world to land it. Being able to do what he loves and hanging with his best friends is what Sheeny enjoys the most about Nitro Circus.

SPOTLIGHT ON

JOSH SHEEHAN

BORN: 2-27-86 **HOME:** Donnybrook, AU ⓞ @sheenyfmx

At the 2019 X Games in Minneapolis, Sheeny won a silver medal in FMX Freestyle and a bronze medal in FMX Best Trick to add to his impressive collection.

Harry Bink was born and raised in Canberra, Australia. At just four years old, Bink attended his first FMX show and was immediately hooked. By 16, Harry dedicated much of his time to becoming a pro FMX rider, undeterred by a schoolteacher telling him to "set realistic goals."

When Harry sets his mind on an objective, watch out. Chances are he will not only accomplish the goal but also surpass it. In just a few short years, Harry Bink has joined the illustrious line of Australian FMX riders who are transforming the sport. After taking the Australian FMX crown in 2015, Bink broke onto the international competition scene in 2016 at both the X Games and X Fighters.

SPOTLIGHT ON
HARRY BINK

BORN: 3-6-94 **HOME:** Canberra, AU ⊙ @harrybink

WORLD'S FIRST

In 2017, Bink made headlines worldwide at the Nitro World Games by landing the world's first frontflip rock solid. Bink's game-changing achievement earned him 1st place honors in FMX Best Trick.

Vice President, Licensing & Publishing Amanda Joiner
Editorial Manager Carrie Bolin

Editor Jessica Firpi
Designer Luis Fuentes
Text Kezia Endsley
Proofreader Rachel Paul
Reprographics Bob Prohaska

Chief Executive Officer Andy Edwards
Chief Commercial Officer Brett Clarke
**Vice President, Global Licensing &
  Consumer Products** Cassie Dombrowski
Vice President, Creative Dov Ribnik
Director, Brand & Athlete Marketing Ricky Melnik
**Account Manager, Global Licensing &
  Consumer Products** Andrew Hogan
Athlete Manager Chris Haffey
Special Thanks Billy Van Vugt, Travis Pastrana

Published by Ripley Publishing 2020

10 9 8 7 6 5 4 3 2 1

Copyright © 2020 Nitro Circus

ISBN: 978-1-60991-387-8

For more information regarding permission, contact:
VP Licensing & Publishing
Ripley Entertainment Inc.
7576 Kingspointe Parkway, Suite 188
Orlando, Florida 32819
Email: publishing@ripleys.com
www.ripleys.com/books

Manufactured in China in March 2020.
First Printing

Library of Congress Control Number: 2020931348

PUBLISHER'S NOTE
While every effort has been made to verify the accuracy of the entries in this book, the Publisher cannot be held responsible for any errors contained in the work. They would be glad to receive any information from readers.

WARNING
Some of the stunts and activities are undertaken by experts and should not be attempted by anyone without adequate training and supervision.

PHOTO CREDITS

COVER Front: Photography by Josh Lynch, Photography by Nicolas Jaquemin, Photography by Drew Ruiz/drp Productions; Back: Photography by Mark Watson; **2** (bc) Photography by Chris Tedesco; **2-3** (bkg) Darren England/ALLSPORT; **3** (br) Brian Bahr/Getty Images; **4-5** (dps) Photography by Nate Christenson; **5** (tr) Photography by Graham Turner, (cr) Photography by Chris Tedesco; **6-7** (dps) Photography by Chris Tedesco, (bkg) © STILLFX/Shutterstock.com; **8** (cl) Photography by Mark Watson; **8-9** (dps) © Vytautas Kielaitis/Shutterstock.com; **12-13** Photography by Mark Watson; **13** (tr) Photography by Josh Lynch, (br) Photography by Chris Tedesco; **14-15** (dps) Photography by Mark Watson; **16** (bl) Photography by Chris Tedesco; **16-17** (dps) © tarczas/Shutterstock.com; **17** (tr) Photography by Mark Watson; **19** (tr) Paul Kane/Getty Images, (cr) Thananuwat Srirasant/Getty Images, (bc) Photography by Mark Watson; **21** (tr) Marty Melville/Getty Images, (cr) Engelke/ullstein bild via Getty Images, (bc) Photography by Chris Tedesco; **22** Photography by Josh Lynch; **23** Photography by Mark Watson; **24** Photography by Mark Watson; **25** Photography by Nicolas Jaquemin; **26** (c) Photography by Chris Tedesco; **27** Photography by Mark Watson; **28** Photography by Mark Watson; **29** Photography by Josh Lynch; **30** Photography by Josh Lynch; **31** Photography by Mark Watson; **32** Photography by Josh Lynch; **34** (tl) Photography by Chris Tedesco, (br) Photography by Josh Lynch; **35** (tr, bl) Photography by Mark Watson; **36** Photography by Josh Lynch; **37** Photography by Mark Watson; **38** Photography by Josh Lynch; **40** Photography by Mark Watson; **42-43** (dps) Photography by Tyler Tate; **44-45** Photography by Mark Watson; **47** Lisa Blumenfeld/Getty Images; **50** Photography by Mark Watson; **51** Photography by Chris Tedesco; **52** Photography by Mark Watson; **53** Photography by Josh Lynch; **55** Photography by Drew Ruiz/drp Productions; **56-57** Photography by Mark Watson; **58** Photography by Mark Watson; **59** Photography by Tyler Tate; **60-61** Photography by Mark Watson; **63** Photography by Chris Tedesco; **MASTER GRAPHICS** Nitro Meter: Created by Luis Fuentes

Key: t = top, b = bottom, c = center, l = left, r = right, sp = single page, dps = double page, bkg = background

All other photos are from Nitro Circus. Every attempt has been made to acknowledge correctly and contact copyright holders, and we apologize in advance for any unintentional errors or omissions, which will be corrected in future editions.